A Child's Introduction to the Early Prophets

BY SHIRLEY NEWMAN

Edited by Louis Newman

Illustrated by Lucille Wallace

Behrman House, Inc. *New York*

To my mother,
Sarah Shulman,
who works tirelessly
for the
children of Israel

To the teacher:

The *Teacher's Guide* to this book is a resource to enhance your own knowledge and skill. It contains overviews of Biblical background and specifies the important ideas of each story. The *Guide* anticipates the students' most challenging questions and includes discussion aids as well as suggestions for class activities. It should be most valuable to lesson preparation.

The Melton Research Center sponsored the first volume in this series of Biblical narratives for children. It is but one of many comprehensive responses to the challenges confronting Jewish education in the United States. This volume reflects the effort to present Biblical content within the Center's educational perspective.

I am deeply grateful to Seymour Rossel for his critical reading of the manuscript and his immeasurable editorial help; to Mrs. Nettie King who supervised the artwork; and to Mrs. Gerry Gould who helped in too many ways to mention. This book is partly theirs.

S.S.N.

Library of Congress Cataloging in Publication Data

Newman, Shirley.
  A child's introduction to the early Prophets.
  SUMMARY: Twenty-eight Bible stories featuring Joshua, Gideon, Samuel, and David.
  1. Bible stories, English—O.T. Former prophets.
[1. Bible stories—O.T. Former prophets] I. Wallace,
Lucille. II. Title.
BS551.2.N45   224'.029'2 [B]   75-14052
ISBN 0-87441-244-7

Published by Behrman House, Inc.
1261 Broadway, New York, N.Y. 10001

Manufactured in the United States of America

10 9 8 7 6 5

Contents

1

God Chooses Joshua

A Story from the Torah

After the Israelite slaves left Egypt, they traveled in the wilderness for forty years. Forty years of living in tents, moving from place to place. Forty years of learning God's laws from Moses, their patient teacher and leader. And forty years of hoping to reach Canaan, where Abraham, Isaac, and Jacob once lived—the land that God had promised to give to the Israelites.

When at last the Israelites came to the Jordan River and could look across and see the green of Canaan, they rejoiced. Soon they would be in the land of their Fathers.

But their happiness was spoiled by one great sadness; Moses, their leader and teacher, would not be going into Canaan with them.

Long before his death, Moses knew that he could never enter the Promised Land because of

5

something that had happened in the wilderness many years before. Setting up their camp at a place called Kadesh, the Israelites had made a frightening discovery: the place had no water!

Afraid and angry, the people blamed Moses and his brother, Aaron, for their troubles.

"We wish we had died rather than come here!" they cried. "Did you bring us to this wilderness so that we and our animals would die here? Did you make us leave Egypt just to come to this terrible place? No grain or fruit grows here—and there is not even any water to drink."

Moses and Aaron did not answer. Instead they begged God to help their troubled people.

And God said to them, "Take the rod that you used in Egypt and call the people together before this rock. Then speak to the rock, saying, 'Pour forth your water.' Water will come rushing from the rock, and the people will have enough for themselves and their animals."

Moses took the rod as God had commanded, and he and Aaron gathered the Israelites in front of the rock. Angrily, Moses said to them, "Listen, you who always say, 'It was better to be slaves in Egypt than to be free in this wilderness!' Do you think we can get water for you out of this rock?"

Still angry, Moses raised his hand and hit the rock twice with the rod. Water poured from the rock, and the people and their animals drank.

But God was not pleased. He said to Moses, "If you had *spoken* to the rock as I asked, the people would have known that it was God who made the rock give forth water. But since you *hit* the rock, they may think that you, with your great strength, made the water flow out. Therefore, because you did not do as I said, you will not lead your people into the land that I have promised them."

But Moses did not leave his people without a leader. When it came time for him to die, he called the Israelites together and spoke to them:

"I am a hundred and twenty years old. I am no longer strong. And God has said to me, 'You shall not go across the Jordan.' So I cannot go with you into Canaan. But do not be afraid. God will help you. You will have the land as He promised. And Joshua will be your leader in my place."

Then Moses called Joshua—the same Joshua who had helped him lead the Israelites in the wilderness—and spoke to him so that all could hear.

"Be strong, and do not be afraid. You will lead our people into the land that God promised our Fathers."

So Joshua became the new leader of the Israelites. He was wise and strong, and the people listened to him and followed him. But never again did the Children of Israel have a leader and teacher like Moses.

2

About the Book of Joshua

It seems that for hundreds of years after Joshua led the Israelites into Canaan, people spoke about what had happened in those days. They told stories about this to their children, who then told them to their children, who told them to *their* children—and so on. Finally, the stories were collected and made into a book. We call it the Book of Joshua.

When stories are passed on this way from one person to another, without being written down, strange things often happen to them. Some parts of the stories usually stay the same no matter how many times they are told, while other parts are changed or forgotten by the storytellers. Most of the time, the storytellers do not know that they have changed or forgotten anything. They believe they are telling the stories exactly as they heard them.

To understand how this happens, let us imagine this:

A boy is walking down the street, when suddenly he hears noises behind him. He looks back and sees three dogs. His heart begins to beat wildly because he is afraid of dogs. Quickly he runs toward the nearest house and hides. After a few minutes, he sees the dogs pass by his hiding place. He waits a long time and comes out only when he is sure that the dogs have gone.

That night the boy tells his younger brother about his adventure. He doesn't change a thing.

One year later, the younger brother decides to write "The Story of My Brother and the Dogs." This is what he writes:

My brother was walking down a quiet street. Suddenly he heard loud barking. He turned around and saw four large dogs running toward him. He could tell that they were getting ready to attack him. So he walked slowly to the nearest house and stepped inside an open garage. When the dogs came close to my brother's hiding place, he saw them stop, paw the ground, and sniff the air trying to find him. But they did not see him because he was too well hidden. Finally they gave up and ran

away. Then my brother came out and went home.

We see how the boy has changed what his older brother told him and we may ask, "Is he lying, or does he really think things happened the way he says they did?"

Our guess is that he is probably not lying, but believes that he is telling exactly what happened. We might say that his memory is playing tricks on him. This often happens when we try to tell about something that took place long ago, or that someone else told us.

Now we may ask another question: "Did the boy tell any parts of the story exactly as they happened?"

The answer, of course, is "Yes, he did."

His brother really did see dogs behind him.

He really did hide.

And the dogs really did go away without hurting him.

So the story that the younger brother wrote is partly true and partly imaginary.

In the same way, many of the stories in the Book of Joshua are probably partly true and partly imaginary.

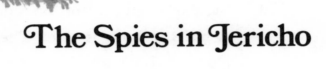

3

The Spies in Jericho

A Story from Joshua

God spoke to Joshua and said, "Moses is dead, and it is time for you to take his place as leader of the Israelites. As Moses told you, *you* will lead the people across the Jordan River to settle in the land of Canaan—the land that I have promised to give them. Be strong, have courage, and always remember one thing:

You must learn well the laws of the Torah that Moses taught in the wilderness. Study these laws, think about them, and live in the way that they teach you. If you do this, I will help you as I helped Moses before you."

Then Joshua went among the people and chose two brave men.

"I am sending you into danger," he said to them. "You are to be spies for your people, and this is what you must do. Leave this camp secretly, without telling anyone that you are going. Find a way to cross the Jordan, and go into Canaan. See what the land is like. Then go into the city of Jericho. Look and listen carefully. After you have learned as much as you can about Canaan, and especially about Jericho, come back quickly and tell me what you have seen and heard."

(At that time, there were many cities in Canaan. Some were fairly large, but most were very small—perhaps only as big as three or four square blocks in the cities of today. Around each city stood a high wall of stone or brick to protect it against attack. Huge gates were built into this wall. They were open in the daytime and closed at night. Every city had its own leader, who was called a "king.")

Now, the spies did as Joshua asked and went into Canaan. There they looked at all they could see and listened to all they could hear. When night came they went to the home of Rahab, a woman of Jericho, and Rahab gave them a place to sleep.

But all did not go smoothly. Some men from the city of Jericho had seen the spies enter Rahab's house, and they ran and told this to the king.

"Israelite spies have come into our city," the men said, "and they are in the house of Rahab. We saw them go in."

So the king of Jericho sent a messenger to Rahab saying, "Bring out the men who are in your house. They are spies sent by the Israelites, who want to destroy our city."

But Rahab did not do what the king wanted.

"Yes, two men did come to my house. But I did not know they were Israelites," she said, pretending to be surprised. "I thought they would spend the night here. But when it began to get dark, they suddenly changed their minds and left the city."

As soon as the messenger rushed away to tell the king, Rahab hurried into the room where the spies were resting.

"Someone saw you come into my house and has told the king about you," she said. "It is not safe for you to stay here any longer. Come with me. I will hide you so that you will not be found if the king should send soldiers to search this house."

Then she led the men up to the flat roof of her house. "Lie down here," she said, pointing to a place on the roof. And she covered them with tall stalks from the flax plant, which had been spread out on her roof to dry. (The Canaanites used this plant to make the cloth called linen.)

Meanwhile, the king of Jericho ordered his

soldiers to chase after the spies and bring them back. Because Rahab had said that the two men had left the city, the soldiers did not bother to search anywhere in Jericho. Instead, they went out through the city gate and hurried toward the Jordan River, hoping to catch the spies before they crossed to the other side.

Now, Rahab's house was built into the wall of the city. Through her window, she watched the soldiers leave, lock the city gate, and run in the direction of the Jordan.

When all was quiet, Rahab went back to the roof.

"Get up," she whispered to the spies. "Get up, for I must speak to you."

The men jumped up quickly, and listened as Rahab spoke. "All the people of this land have heard how God took you out of Egypt, and how He helped you destroy those who tried to harm you in the wilderness," she said. "I know that the Israelites will soon conquer our city, and I am afraid. So I must ask you to make me a promise. Since I have been kind to you, promise me that you will be kind to me and to all my family—my father, my mother, my sisters, and my brothers. Promise me that you will save our lives as I have saved yours."

The men promised, and they followed Rahab back into her house. Here, she picked up a long rope. Holding one end tightly, she dropped the other end through her window until it reached the ground outside the city wall.

When she had helped the two men slide down the rope, she said to them, "Do not go to the Jordan. Instead, run toward the mountains and hide there for three days. After that, it will be safe for you to go back to the Israelite camp."

"We thank you," the spies said. "And this is how you can help us save you when we come into your city. Tie a red cord to the window through which you just let us down. Then bring everyone in your family into your house. Let nobody go outside, and do not tell anyone that we were here."

"So it will be," Rahab said, and she sent them off.

The Israelites headed toward the mountains, and Rahab tied a red cord to her window.

When three days had passed, the two spies made their way back to the Israelite camp. They told Joshua all they had seen and heard, and everything that had happened to them in the house of Rahab.

4

About the Land of Canaan

Before we read another story from the Book of Joshua, let us stop and learn some important facts—facts about:

> The land of Canaan.
> The people of Canaan—the Canaanites.
> The Children of Israel—the Israelites.

What was Canaan like when the Israelites came there?

Did it have much water, or was it dry?
Was it low and flat, or covered with hills and mountains?
What crops grew in its soil?

Canaan was a tiny country. Within it there were cold, snow-covered mountains and hot, jungle-like valleys; high hills, as well as the lowest place on earth; thick forests and open, grassy plains; swamps where the ground was as full of water as a wet sponge, and dry, rocky wilderness where rain seldom fell. Canaan was like a patchwork quilt made up of many different pieces of cloth laid side by side and sewn together.

If Joshua and the Israelites could have looked down on this little country from somewhere high above the earth, these are some of the things they would have seen:

Canaan's western boundary was formed by the Mediterranean Sea. Along its smooth, curving coastline lay a narrow ribbon of land called the Coastal Plain. This land was flat and had a good supply of water. Crops grew well in its rich, dark soil. There were also many towns and cities on the Coastal Plain.

To the east of the Coastal Plain was the Hill Country, a strip of tall mountains and rolling hills stretching down the length of Canaan. Some of the hills were covered with forests.

On the side of the Hill Country nearest the Coastal Plain, cool breezes blew, the soil was good, and there was usually plenty of rain. Much of this

land was used for farming and for raising sheep, goats, and cattle. Olive trees, fig trees, and grapevines grew on the hillsides. Wheat and other grains grew in the valleys that lay among the mountains.

But in some sections of the Hill Country farthest from the Coastal Plain, the land changed. The green, rolling areas where rain fell suddenly turned into bare cliffs of brown, gray, and white stone. In this dry, wild part of the Hill Country almost nothing grew, and the sun burned hot all year round.

East of the Hill Country was the Jordan Valley, the land along the banks of the Jordan River. For most of its length, this valley was divided into two levels, like steps—the lower one next to the river, and the higher one farther back. These two levels were separated by a line of chalky gray hills on which nothing grew. Much of the upper valley was used for farming and for pasturing animals. There were also cities and towns there. But a good part of the lower level was covered by a thick, dark-green jungle of trees, bushes, and vines. No people lived on the lower level. The weather in the Jordan Valley was always hot.

At the eastern edge of the valley flowed the Jordan River. It was a small river that started in the far north of Canaan, near snow-covered Mount Hermon, the tallest mountain in the country.

At the foot of Mount Hermon, a little stream rushed out of a cave in the side of a cliff. Farther on, it was joined by another stream, and then by two more. As if happy to be with one another, these four flowed on as one and became the Jordan River.

At first the narrow little river moved along peacefully. But soon it began to rush and tumble in a downhill path, twisting and turning through the land. Along the way it was joined by other streams that flowed into it from either side. Each new addition made it wider and stronger. (However, it never became *very* wide. It was not like the Nile, or the Mississippi, or other great rivers of the world.)

As the Jordan dashed ahead, it tore up huge clumps of earth, carrying them away in its swiftly moving waters; the clear little mountain stream became a brown, muddy river.

Finally the restless Jordan came to the Dead Sea—the lowest spot in the world. Here it flowed into the sea and stopped its wanderings.

In the southern part of Canaan lay the Negev, the wilderness where Abraham and Isaac once roamed with their flocks. This land was covered with rocks and sands of many colors—blacks, browns, grays, reds, purples, yellows—like a strange, wild painting. From time to time, patches of grass and trees suddenly appeared in the midst of all this dryness. Each green spot was called an oasis. Some oases were small while others were large. They were usually watered by streams that flowed underground.

In the Negev, water was more precious than gold. Over the years, the people of the Negev had learned to collect and save every little bit of rain that fell. They made huge holes in the rocks or in the ground so rainwater could flow in and be stored. These storage places were called cisterns. Sometimes enough water was gathered in a cistern to supply the people through several dry years.

5

About the Canaanites

In this land of many differences lived a people called the Canaanites. Historians and archaeologists—men and women who study the past—have discovered much about how the Canaanites lived.

At the time that the Israelites crossed the Jordan, most Canaanites were farmers. They lived mainly on the plains and in the valleys—the flat, open parts of Canaan. Very few made their homes in the hills or mountains.

The Canaanite farmers grew wheat, barley, grapes, olives, figs, and dates. Some also raised cattle, sheep, and goats.

The Canaanites worshiped many gods. They thought that their gods looked and acted like human beings—eating and drinking, loving and hating, feeling happy or sad. The best known of their gods were Ba'al and his wife, Anat.

The Canaanites made many statues of these "gods-in-the-shape-of-people." We call these statues idols. The Canaanites bowed down before the idols and prayed to them. Many of these idols have been found by archaeologists and can be seen in museums.

In Canaan, as in all farming communities, there were times when the crops did not grow well and there was not enough food for the people. The Canaanites believed that this happened when Ba'al and his wife became angry with them. So in order to keep the gods happy, the farmers brought them gifts—animals, birds, fruits, vegetables, and grains. The animals and birds were burned on altars of stone. This kind of gift is called a *sacrifice.*

The Canaanites believed that the gods did not care how the people acted toward one another —whether they were kind or cruel, honest or dishonest, loving or full of hatred. They were sure that their gods wanted nothing from them except gifts and sacrifices.

Many Canaanites thought the best gift that one could give to the gods was a child. Therefore, parents sometimes sacrificed their own children on the altars.

Although the Israelites also thought that God wanted them to bring Him sacrifices, they did not believe that this was *all* He wanted of them. Moses had taught the Israelites over and over again that they could not please God unless they acted toward each other as He wanted them to.

In the Torah, we read that Moses had especially warned the Israelites not to learn the ways of the Canaanites after they crossed the Jordan:

> Do not ask about their gods, saying, "How did those nations worship their gods? I, too, will do the same." You shall not act this way toward the Lord your God, for they did for their gods every horrible thing that God hates, even burning their sons and daughters in sacrifice to their gods.

And Moses had reminded them again of what they *should* do:

> For I command you this day to love the Lord your God—to walk in His ways, and to keep His commandments, His laws, and His rules. Then God will bless you and you will live happily in the land you are about to enter.

6

About the Israelites

The Israelites who came into the farming country of Canaan were wandering shepherds. They grew no crops but found food and water as they moved from place to place, living in tents and pasturing their flocks of sheep and goats as they traveled through the wilderness.

The Israelites were divided into groups called tribes. Each tribe was like a very, very large family. We usually say that there were *twelve* Israelite tribes.

Two tribes were named after the two sons of Joseph—

Ephraim and Manasseh.

The rest were called by the names of Jacob's sons—

Asher, Benjamin, Dan,
Gad, Issacher, Judah,
Levi, Napthali, Reuben,
Simeon, and Zebulun.

Joseph was the only one of Jacob's sons who had no tribe named for him.

If you count the names above, you will discover that *thirteen* tribes are listed. But a moment ago we said there were only twelve tribes. How can there be thirteen and twelve at the same time?

Here is the answer to this puzzle.

After the Israelites settled in Canaan, the land was divided into twelve parts—called tribal lands. Each tribe lived in its own section: Asher lived in the tribal land of Asher; Dan in the tribal land of Dan; Judah in its section, and so on.

But the thirteenth, the tribe of Levi, did not have its own section of Canaan. Instead, each of the other tribes set aside some cities, along with the fields around them, for the Levites, as the people of Levi were called. Altogether there were forty-eight such cities. So the Levites spread out among all the tribal lands instead of living separately like the other tribes of Israel. That is why we speak of *twelve* Israelite tribes instead of thirteen.

Of these twelve tribes two and a half lived on one side of the Jordan River and nine and a half lived on the other. Reuben, Gad, and half of the tribe of Manasseh were on the *eastern* side of the river—the side from which Moses had looked across into Canaan before he died. The others were on the *western* side. Does this mean that two and a

25

half tribes never crossed the Jordan with the rest of the Israelites?

In the Torah, there is a story that gives an answer to this:

> As the Israelites moved along on their way to the Jordan River, they came to a place that was very good for raising animals.
>
> "How we wish we could settle here," thought the people of Reuben and Gad, "for we own large numbers of sheep and goats."
>
> So the men of these tribes went to Moses and said, "If you let us make our home on this land, we will build shelters to protect our animals, and towns to protect our wives and children. Then we shall leave our families and cross the Jordan with the rest of the Israelites. If they have to fight, we shall help them. And we will not come back here until every one of them has found a place to live."

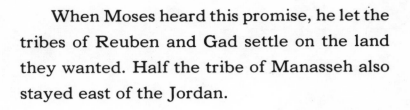

When Moses heard this promise, he let the tribes of Reuben and Gad settle on the land they wanted. Half the tribe of Manasseh also stayed east of the Jordan.

Most of the Canaanites were farmers, and most of the Israelites were shepherds. They were different in other important ways, too.

The Israelites believed there was only one God, while the Canaanites thought that there were many gods.

The Israelites believed that God has no shape or form, while the Canaanites thought that gods looked like people.

And—perhaps most important of all—the Israelites believed that God cares about how people act toward one another, while the Canaanites did not think their gods cared about this. The Israelites learned that God wanted them to be good to the poor and to strangers; to pay workers their wages at the end of each day; to be respectful and kind to old people; and to use honest weights and measures in their marketplaces.

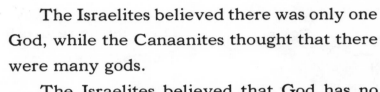

7

The Israelites in Canaan

Now, let us return to the stories of the Book of Joshua.

For three days, the Israelites waited beside the Jordan. On the other side they could see the land of Canaan. But the river was deep. How could they get across with all of their children and animals?

Their question was answered on the third day, and the answer had to do with the Ark.

"The Ark, a beautiful box of wood covered with gold, was the most precious treasure of the Israelite tribes, for inside it were the two stone tablets on which the Ten Commandments were written. Usually the Ark stood in a special tent called the *Mishkan*. When the Israelites moved from one place to another, it was carried carefully on the shoulders of priests—men from the tribe of Levi."

On the third day, the leaders of the Israelites

came through the camp saying, "Soon the Ark will pass by here. When the Ark passes by, you must follow it."

So the people folded their tents, packed their belongings, and waited. Before long they saw the Ark being carried by, and they followed as they had been told to do. Slowly the people walked to the very edge of the Jordan—first the priests carrying the Ark, and then all the men, women, and children of the Israelite tribes.

At the river's edge, Joshua spoke to the Israelites, saying:

From this you will know that God will help you as He promised. As you watch, the priests who are carrying the Ark will walk into the Jordan. And the moment their feet touch the muddy river bottom, the water of the Jordan will stop moving. Instead of flowing as it always does, the water will pile up in one enormous heap!

And so it was. As the Israelites watched, the priests carrying the Ark stepped carefully into the river. No sooner did their feet touch the water, than the Jordan stopped flowing. The people could see the water piling up far away until it looked like a tall, wet mountain. And right in front of them a wide, dry path opened across the riverbed. On this path, the Israelites walked into Canaan. Only the priests did not move from where they stood.

When all the people had crossed, God said to Joshua, "Choose twelve men and say to them, 'Each of you is to take one stone out of the Jordan and bring it to the place where we will rest tonight.'" So Joshua chose twelve men and spoke to them as God had commanded.

Then Joshua called to the priests, "Come out of the river." And as soon as the priests stepped upon the shore, the piled-up water of the Jordan tumbled back into place, and the river flowed on as before.

That night the Israelites stopped near the city of Jericho. When the people had made their camp, Joshua set up the twelve stones that had been taken from the Jordan. Then he said to the Israelites, "When your children ask you, in years to come, 'Why are these stones here?' you shall say to them:

These stones come from the bottom of the

Jordan river. They are *reminders*. Whenever we look at them, we remember that God did us a great kindness. He dried up the water of the Jordan so that we could walk across into the land of Canaan.

The following day, the Israelites waited in their tents outside the walled city of Jericho. Before long, Joshua spoke to them. First he turned to the priests and said, "Soon you will be carrying the Ark once more. But this time seven other priests, carrying seven rams' horns, will walk in front of you." Then he spoke to the people. "For six days you will walk around the wall of Jericho, *once each day*. The Ark will go before you. And before the Ark will go seven priests carrying seven rams' horns. As you walk, no sound must come out of your lips. Only listen quietly to the voice of the rams' horns. But on the seventh day I shall call out to you, 'Shout!' Then you shall shout with all your strength."

So the priests and the Israelites walked around the city of Jericho as Joshua had ordered. No one said a word. No one made a sound. Only the blowing of the rams' horns was heard. For six days the people walked around the city, once each day.

Early on the morning of the seventh day, they began to walk once more. They made no sound, and again the rams' horns blew. But on this day

they circled Jericho seven times instead of just once. And on the seventh time around, Joshua called out to the people, "Shout!"

And the people shouted a great and deafening shout! And as they shouted, another sound started to fill the air—the roar of hundreds of enormous bricks crashing and tumbling one over another. The wall of Jericho was falling to the ground!

Then the Israelites climbed over the fallen wall and captured the city, killing every man, woman and child. And Jericho was completely destroyed. Only Rahab and her family were left alive.

Over many years, Joshua and the Israelites fought more battles and captured more cities in Canaan. But there came a time when Joshua was old, and he knew that he would soon die. He had done much to help his people, but there was still much more to be done. Although a few of the tribes had already found homes in the land, some did not yet have places to live. They were still wanderers. So Joshua spoke to the Israelite leaders and told them which part of Canaan would someday belong to each tribe.

After this, Joshua called all the Israelites together and spoke to them:

Always remember what God has done for you.

He brought Abraham into Canaan and promised to give this land to his children's children. He brought your fathers and mothers out of Egypt and saved them from Pharaoh. And He brought *you* back to Canaan and helped you to fight against those who would not let you make your home here.

In Canaan He gave you cities to live in and fields in which to grow food. *You did not win these with your own strength. It was God who helped you win them.*

Therefore you must not turn to the gods of the people around you. You must serve only the God of your Fathers. You must follow the laws and commandments that Moses taught, so that you may live as God wants you to.

Do not learn the ways of the Canaanites, though many still live in the land. Do not make marriages with them. For if you do these things and forget God's laws, He will not let you stay in the land that He has given you.

And the Israelites answered Joshua:

We remember all the good that God did for our Fathers and for us. He brought us out of Egypt and made us free. He took care of us in the wilderness, and He gave us the land of Canaan. Therefore we shall walk in His ways, and not worship other gods.

Joshua died, and for the first time since the Israelite tribes had left Egypt, they had no leader. There was no one to remind them to "walk in God's ways," or to help them when they had troubles.

Becoming Different

Much of the Book of Joshua tells about the wars that the Israelites fought in Canaan. These war stories are not very pleasant. If you read them, you may feel upset and unhappy. You may say to yourself, "What cruel things the Israelite soldiers did! Did they *really* act this way, or did someone make up these parts of the stories?"

The answer is that when they fought against the Canaanites, the Israelite soldiers probably did act cruelly—in the same way as other soldiers of those days.

What could have made them behave this way? To try to understand this, we must remember something very important. The Israelites, whom we now call the Jewish people, were a very *young* people when they came into Canaan. They were like children growing up. They still had much to learn about how human beings should behave toward each other. In some ways, the Israelites had already learned to be more grown up than many other people of their time. For instance, they were different from the Canaanites, who burned children on altars as sacrifices to their gods. Moses had taught the Israelites that this was wrong and that God did not want them to do it. However, in fighting wars, it seems that the Israelites acted like their neighbors.

You may want to ask another question: "Why did the teacher who wrote the Book of Joshua think it was important to tell the history and the stories of a time when the Israelites still had so much to learn? Why did he choose to write down and save stories in which whole cities and all their people were destroyed by our ancestors?"

The teacher does not give us his reasons in the book, but we can guess at an answer. To do this, let us pretend that we are the teacher. Let us imagine what he may have been thinking when, long after Joshua's death, he decided to put together the Book of Joshua.

We are a small nation, and our people know they are newcomers to this land. They know that their leaders had faith in God. They know that their ancestors fought many battles to settle in this land. They also know that their ancestors destroyed many cities and killed

many people. They tell stories about these things. They love to hear these stories. They tell them over and over again. I think the Israelites will always remember these stories and the exciting victories they tell about. But what else will the Israelites say about their past? What *reasons* will they give for Joshua's victories? How will they explain the conquest of Canaan? Will they boast about what good soldiers their great-great-great grandparents were? Will they teach their children to love war? Will they believe that God wants them always to be warriors?

The people of Israel must not do any of these things. In this book, I must teach them the *real* reason for the victory of Joshua and his people. I must make them understand that their ancestors did not manage to come into this land and settle it because of their own strength but *because of God's help*. I must also teach them that God does not want wars, and that this war was a special case. They must understand that there was a special reason why God let the Israelites take Canaan away from the people who lived there. It was because the Canaanites were so cruel and did so many hateful things. God punished them by taking their land away from them and destroying many of them. Then, I must remind the

Israelites that if *they* begin to act as the Canaanites did, they, too, will be driven from the land.

Last of all, I must teach the Israelites why Joshua led the people to victory. It was not because he was a great general. *It was because he followed the teachings of Moses and served God.* That is why he was given the privilege of leading our ancestors across the Jordan into Canaan, just as Moses had led their fathers and mothers across the Sea of Reeds.

Above all, the teacher who wrote the Book of Joshua wanted the Israelites to learn that all the unusual and helpful things that happened in their past took place *for one important reason.* He repeated it over and over again. The reason was that God wanted to have a people—the Children of Israel, the Jewish people—who would live according to the Torah's teachings. That is why, in the Book of Joshua, God says, "The Torah must never leave your lips. You must think about it and talk about it by day and by night."

If the author of the Book of Joshua were using the words we use today, he might have said,

"Don't think you are great. You are in this country because God wants a Torah-following people."

9

The Israelites Forget

Earlier, we learned about the Torah and now about the Book of Joshua. Both of these are part of a much larger book known as the Bible.

The Bible is made up of many small books. First there is the Torah; next, the Book of Joshua; and after that, the Book of Judges. These are followed by other books whose names you will learn as you go on studying. But now we shall talk only about the Book of Judges for a while.

In this book, we shall read about some of the attacks that were made upon the Israelite tribes after they settled in Canaan. We will also read about the Israelite leaders who helped the tribes defend themselves against those who wanted to destroy them or take away their freedom or their homes. The Israelites called these leaders *judges*. They believed that the judges were sent by God to save them in times of danger, and to lead them when there was peace. They told many stories about their judges and the great deeds they did.

After a long time, these stories, like the stories in the Book of Joshua, were collected and written down.

You may remember when we talked about the Book of Joshua, we said that many of its stories were probably partly true and partly imaginary. It seems that the Book of Judges also contains many stories that are partly true and partly imaginary.

Even after all the tribes were finally settled in Canaan, the Israelites were not the only people living there. Throughout the land there were still many Canaanites.

Some lived in the cities that had been too strong for the Israelites to conquer, such as Jerusalem.

Some stayed on in the Hill Country where most of the Israelites settled. These Canaanites were often friendly to the newcomers from the wilderness.

Some Canaanites lived in the low, flat valleys and on the Coastal Plain. (Not many Israelites had tried to find homes for themselves in these places. Most of them feared that if there was fighting, their soldiers, on foot, could not win against the Canaanites of the plains and valleys, who often rode into battle in horse-drawn chariots. It was easier for them to fight in the hills and mountains,

where their enemies, the Canaanites, would also have to fight on foot—where chariots could not travel safely over the uneven, rocky ground.)

In Canaan, life was hard for the Israelites. Before coming here, they had been wandering shepherds setting up their tents wherever they found food and water for themselves and their animals. But now most of them became farmers, and they had to learn many things that wandering shepherds did not know. How to build houses and towns. How to plow, plant, and harvest. How to store grain in the years when the harvest was good, so there would be enough to eat in the years when the harvest was poor.

The Israelite shepherds learned all this and more, and in time, most of them became good farmers.

The Israelites learned, but they also forgot.

In the wilderness, Moses had taught them that there is only *one* God—a God who cannot be seen—who made heaven and earth and everything in them. Moses had taught them that it was this God—the God of Abraham, Isaac, and Jacob—who brought the Israelites out of slavery and made them free.

And Moses had also taught the Israelites laws and commandments, so they would know how God wanted them to live. Both Moses and Joshua had said to them, "Do not learn the ways of the Canaanites."

But many Israelites forgot what they had been taught. They *did* learn the ways of the Canaanites among whom they lived. They learned to worship the gods of the land and to act like the people of the land. Another way of saying this is that the Israelites became assimilated in Canaan.

Over and over, the Israelites forgot the ways of God—the laws and commandments that Moses had taught their ancestors in the wilderness. They made statues of silver, gold, wood, and stone, and they called these gods. They stole from each other, hurt each other, and killed each other.

Everyone did as he pleased. There was no leader to say, "It is wrong for Israelites to do such things." There was no one to teach the people what God expected of them, as Moses had done in his time.

For many, many years after they settled in Canaan, the Israelites had no peace. From time to time, one tribe or another was attacked and had to fight for its land and for the lives of its people. The attackers came from many places—from outside Canaan as well as from within.

During their years in the wilderness, the Is-

raelite tribes had lived together and, when necessary, had fought together. They were one people. Now each tribe lived on its own land and took care of its own needs. Some of the tribal lands were far from each other, and the lands of unfriendly neighbors lay between them. It was dangerous to pass through these lands. So in Canaan, the Israelites were no longer one people. And sometimes they did not even help one another in times of war or other trouble.

As you read the stories from the Book of Judges, you may say to yourself, "Since we learned that both the stories in the Torah and the stories in the Book of Joshua teach lessons and ideas that the writer wanted the Jewish people to remember, the same is probably also true of the stories in the Book of Judges. Now, what lessons may the stories of the judges be trying to teach?" One lesson seems to be:

If the Jewish people forget the laws and commandments that Moses taught—if they do not "walk in the ways of God"—then God will punish them. They will not be strong and safe in their own land.

But if they see that they have done wrong and change their ways, God will forgive them and protect them once more.

10

A Mother in Israel

The Story of Deborah

The Israelites had forgotten the ways of God. So Jabin, the king of the Canaanite city of Hazor, conquered them.

Now, Jabin had nine hundred chariots of iron. With his chariots and his men, he fought against the Israelites and defeated them. For twenty years, Jabin ruled over them and made their life very hard.

When the Israelites could no longer bear their troubles, they remembered the God of their Fathers and cried out to Him for help.

At that time, there lived a judge named Deborah in the Hill Country of the tribe of Ephraim. Some called her a "Mother in Israel." Each day Deborah sat in the shade of a tall palm tree called "the Tree of Deborah," and Israelites came to her from many places. They brought her questions they could not answer and arguments they could not settle, and she tried to help them.

Deborah knew how much her people suffered because of Jabin. She knew that even travelers on the highways were not safe from attack by his soldiers. Israelites who had to go from one part of the land to another tried to find little out-of-the-way roads or twisting forest paths so they would not be seen as they moved along.

One day Deborah sent for Barak, of the tribe of Naftali, and told him, "This is what God has said: 'You are to take ten thousand men and go with them to the mountain called Tabor. There, near the river, I will bring Sisera, the general of Jabin's army, with the king's chariots and soldiers. You and your soldiers will fight against the army of Sisera—and you will win!'"

But Barak was afraid. He said to Deborah, "If you come with me, I will go. But if you do not, I will not go."

Deborah answered, "I will go with you, but this will not bring you honor. People will say that God let a woman defeat Sisera."

Then Barak gathered ten thousand men, and Deborah went with them to Mount Tabor.

When Sisera heard that Barak and his men were at Tabor, he gathered his nine hundred chariots of iron and all his soldiers, and he brought them to the river that flowed near the mountain.

And Deborah said to Barak, "On this day, God will help you win against Sisera."

Barak went down from Mount Tabor, leading his ten thousand men. At the foot of the mountain, they began to attack Sisera's army.

Suddenly a strange thing happened. Sisera's soldiers became frightened and began to run away, some on foot and some in their chariots. Strangest of all was Sisera himself. He climbed down from his chariot and ran.

Barak and the Israelites chased after Sisera's soldiers and killed them all.

Sisera alone escaped. Tired and afraid, he came to the tent of a woman named Yael, who was not an Israelite. And Yael said to him, "Come in, and do not be frightened."

So Sisera went into the tent and lay down to rest.

Still afraid, he said to Yael, "Stand near the door of the tent while I sleep, and if anyone comes and asks, 'Is there a man here?' say, 'No, there is not.'"

But Sisera did not know that Yael was a friend of the Israelites, and that she wanted to help them free themselves from king Jabin and his army. She wanted to help so much, that while Sisera slept, she crept up behind him and killed him.

When Yael saw Barak walking toward her tent, she called to him: "Come in and I will show you the man you are looking for."

When the fighting was over, Deborah, the Judge, sang a song of thanks and of anger: thanks to God for freeing the Israelites from Jabin; thanks to the tribes that sent men to help Barak; and anger at the tribes that sent no help at all.

And of Yael, friend of the Israelites, Deborah sang:

May Yael be greatly blessed.
The most blessed of women may she be—
more blessed than all women who live in tents.

And there was peace in the land for forty years.

11

Gideon Trusts God

Once more the Israelites forgot what Moses and Joshua had taught them. Again they began to worship the gods of Canaan and to act like the people of Canaan.

And the Midianites—tent people who lived in the wilderness across the Jordan—attacked the Israelites and made them afraid.

Every year, the Midianites came into Canaan to steal the Israelites' crops, take their animals, and destroy their fields. Year after year they came, attacked, and left—only to return another time.

The Israelites became very poor because of this. And in their trouble they remembered God and cried out to Him for help. God heard their cries and had pity on them.

One day during the wheat harvest, Gideon, a farmer from the tribe of Manasseh, was beating out some wheat in his wine-press, the place where grapes were made into wine. (He hoped that the Midianites would not think of looking for wheat where there should be wine. Perhaps in this way he could hide some of his crop to use for the coming year.)

Suddenly a messenger of God appeared before him and said, "God is with you, O great soldier."

Gideon smiled sadly.

"If God is with us," he said, "why has all this happened to us? And where are God's great deeds, which our Fathers have told us about? Why does He not show us one of His great deeds now? Why does He let the Midianites oppress us so?"

The messenger acted as if he had not heard Gideon's questions.

"Gideon," he said, "God has chosen *you* to save the Israelites from the Midianites."

Again Gideon smiled, but his voice was even sadder than before.

"How can *I* save Israel?" he asked. "I am not a powerful man. My family is the poorest in the tribe of Manasseh, and I am the least important one in my family."

"God will help you," the messenger answered, "and you will defeat the Midianites."

That night, Gideon heard the voice of God saying, "Gideon, go out and break the altar on which the people of this city burn sacrifices to the Canaanite god Ba'al. And destroy the wooden post beside it, where they worship the goddess Asherah."

And Gideon went out into the darkness and obeyed God's command.

The next morning, when the men of Gideon's city saw what had happened, they could hardly believe their eyes.

"Who did this?" they asked. They searched until they found the answer. "It was Gideon, son of Joash."

The men of the city went to Gideon's father and said, "Bring out your son. He must die for what he did!"

But Joash would not give them his son. "Must *you* fight for Ba'al?" he replied. "If Ba'al is truly a god, then let him fight for himself."

The men listened, and they did not harm Gideon.

Not long afterward, a great army of Midianites crossed the Jordan and camped in the Valley of Jezreel, a broad, grassy valley in Canaan. They were ready to attack the Israelites again. Soon they would swoop down upon farms and towns, stealing or destroying everything in sight, as they had done many times before.

When Gideon heard that the Midianites were in Canaan, he remembered what the messenger of God had told him. He must save the Israelites!

So Gideon sent people to some of the nearby tribes, saying, "We shall no longer let the Midianites harm us as they have done for so many years. I am ready to fight against them. Let all who can help, come and join me."

Thousands and thousands of Israelites came to Gideon.

Gideon looked at the gathered men, and suddenly became worried. "Does God *really* want me to lead them against the Midianites? Will God *really* help us? Can I trust Him?"

And Gideon said to God, "I am not sure that You will save us from the Midianites. I must ask You to prove that You will keep Your word."

Then Gideon took some thick wool and placed it on the ground. He spoke to God again. "I shall leave this wool here all night. In the morning, I shall come back to look at it. If the wool is wet with dew, and all the ground is dry, I will know that You are really going to help me."

When he came back early the next morning, the sign he had asked for was there. The wool was soaking wet, but the ground was dry.

But still Gideon was not sure. He said to God, "Please do not be angry with me, but I must test You once more. I will leave the wool on the ground overnight again. This time, let the wool stay dry while all the ground is wet with dew."

And God let Gideon test Him a second time.

The next morning, the ground was soaking wet, and the wool was dry.

Now Gideon trusted God, and he got ready to lead his army against the Midianites.

12

Gideon Defeats the Midianites

The next day Gideon, together with all the people who had come to help, set up camp on the side of a mountain near the Jezreel Valley, where the Midianites had made their camp.

Then God spoke to Gideon: "There are too many people with you. If you go against the Midianites with this great army, the people of Israel might think, 'It is because of our own strength that we defeated the Midianites.' Therefore, say to your men, 'If anyone is afraid, let him go home.'"

Gideon did as God asked, and twenty-two thousand men left. Only ten thousand remained.

But God spoke to Gideon again. "There are still too many with you. This is what you must do next. Take all of your army down to the water. There I will tell you how to choose who is to go with you and who is to stay behind."

Gideon took his army to the water and waited.

"Now," God said, "let the men drink from the stream, and as they do, watch each one carefully. If a man scoops up water in his cupped hands and laps it with his tongue, as a dog laps water, you are to take him with you. But if he gets down on his knees and leans over to drink right from the stream, send him away."

Gideon watched as the men drank. And of the ten thousand, only three hundred scooped up water in their cupped hands and lapped with their tongues.

"Take the three hundred," God commanded Gideon. "With this small army I will save the Israelites from the Midianites."

And the three hundred went back to their camp on the mountainside.

In the middle of that night, God woke Gideon and said to him, "Awake! It is time to attack the Midianites. I will help you defeat them so that they will never again bring trouble to the Israelites."

But God saw that Gideon was still afraid, so He said, "If you fear to begin the battle right now, go down first with Purah, your servant, to the Midianite camp. Go there quietly and listen to what the soldiers are saying. The words that you will hear will make your fright go away, and you will feel strong enough to lead your men against the Midianites."

So Gideon and Purah, his servant, went down in the darkness and crept up to the edge of the

Midianite camp. From their hiding place, they could see tents, camels, and soldiers—thousands and thousands of soldiers.

Gideon and Purah listened, and they heard a soldier telling a dream to his friend. "I dreamed that a round, hard loaf of bread came tumbling into our camp. The loaf struck a tent and turned it upside down, and the tent fell flat on the ground."

Then the other soldier said, "I know the meaning of your dream. The loaf of bread stands for the sword of Gideon, the Israelite. Soon God will help him strike the army of Midian with his sword and defeat us."

When Gideon heard the dream and its meaning, he thanked God and quickly went back to the Israelite camp.

"Wake up, for God is about to help you defeat the powerful Midianites!" he called to his men.

Gideon then divided the men into three groups. To each man he gave three things: a ram's horn, an empty pitcher, and a burning torch to hide inside the pitcher.

"Now follow me down the mountain," he said, "and when we get near the Midianite camp, watch me carefully. Whatever I do, you must do too."

Without a sound, the Israelites came down the mountain and stood near the camp of the sleeping Midianites. They watched Gideon—ready to do whatever he did.

Suddenly the night stillness was broken. Gideon and his three hundred men were blowing their horns, smashing their pitchers with a great noise, waving their burning torches high in the air, and shouting as loudly as they could.

Awakened by the horrible noise, the Midianite soldiers stumbled out of their tents, confused and sleepy. "We are being attacked!" they screamed. Many ran through the camp trying to find the enemy. But in the darkness, they found only each other, and Midianite killed Midianite by mistake. Those who were left alive tried to run away, but the Israelites found them and killed every one.

Afterward, the leaders of the tribes of Israel came to Gideon and said, "Rule over us—you, and your son, and your son's son—for you have saved us from the Midianites."

But Gideon would not be their king. "I will not rule over you," he said, "and neither will my son. God will be your king."

Then Gideon became a judge, and he continued to help the Israelites all the days of his life.

For a time the Israelites did not turn to the gods of the Canaanites and to the ways of the Canaanites. They turned back to God, the God of their Fathers, and remembered His laws and commandments.

13

A Stubborn Man

It seemed as if the Israelites would never learn. Still another time they left the ways of God and began to act like the Canaanites. And another of the neighboring peoples attacked them and took away their freedom. This time it was the Philistines who began to rule over Israel. They were a cruel and frightening enemy.

Very soon after the Israelites had crossed the Jordan into the eastern part of Canaan, the Philistines had entered the western part of the land. The Philistines came from an island somewhere near the European country of Greece. After crossing the Mediterranean Sea in well-built ships, they had landed on the western shore of Canaan and settled on the Coastal Plain, where they built five strong cities. Each of these was ruled by a Philistine king. Soon all their Canaanite neighbors began to fear the Philistines.

These new settlers had brought with them a secret that helped them in both peace and war: they knew how to make iron. This was something that neither the Canaanites nor the Israelites knew how to do. The Philistines did not share their secret with anyone else in Canaan, and so for a long time they were the only ones there who *made* this metal. Others in Canaan who used iron (such as Jabin, king of Hazor, about whom we read in the story of Deborah) probably had to buy the iron and bring it into Canaan from lands where iron was made.

The Story of Samson

In the days when the Philistines ruled over the Israelites, there lived in the tribe of Dan a man named Manoah, who had no children. One morning a messenger of God came to Manoah's wife and said, "Soon you will have a son. But you are not to treat him as you would treat any other child. You are to treat him in a special way: *You must never cut his hair.* When your son grows up, he will help to save Israel from the cruel Philistine rulers."

When the messenger finished speaking, the woman ran home and told her husband what had just happened. "A messenger of God came to me!" she said breathlessly. "He told me, 'Soon you will give birth to a son.'"

A few months later, a child was born to Manoah and his wife, and they named him Samson. As Samson grew, his strength grew, until he was strong enough to tear a lion apart with his hands.

When Samson was a young man, he visited a town not far from his home. He saw a Philistine woman there and fell in love with her.

"Get me that woman to be my wife," he said to his mother and father.

"Why must you take a Philistine woman as your wife?" his parents asked. "Is there no woman among the Israelites whom you can marry?"

But Samson would not listen. "Get me the wife I asked for," he said stubbornly, "for she is the one I like."

So Samson's parents did as he asked, and the Philistine woman became his wife.

After the wedding, Samson had a party for the young men of the town. Thirty Philistines, neighbors of his wife's family, came to celebrate with him. When they were all eating, drinking, and enjoying themselves, Samson said to his guests, "I have a riddle for you. If you tell me the right answer within the next seven days. I will give each of you a set of beautiful new clothes. But if you do not find the answer, then each of you must give *me* a set of new clothes."

"Tell us your riddle," the young men said. And Samson did.

For six days, the thirty Philistines thought and thought about Samson's riddle, but they could not find the answer. On the seventh day, they went to Samson's wife and said, "We do not want to give your husband the clothes we promised him. Therefore, before this day is finished, *you* must find out the answer to his riddle and tell it to us. If you do not, we will kill you and your whole family."

When the men had left, Samson's wife came to him in tears. "You do not love me," she said, "and this is how I know. At your wedding party, you told your guests a riddle and asked them to bring you an answer within the next seven days. But you did not tell *me* the answer. That means you do not trust me."

"I did not even tell the answer to my mother and father," Samson replied angrily. "So why should I tell you?"

But Samson's wife would not leave him in peace. Over and over she asked Samson for the riddle's answer, until at last he told her.

After she told the thirty Philistines the answer, they brought it to Samson.

"You got this from my wife!" he shouted.

Samson's heart was filled with anger, and great

strength came into his body. He ran to a nearby city, where he killed thirty Philistines, took their clothes, and gave the clothes to the men who had answered his riddle.

Still angry, Samson left his wife and went back to live in his father's house.

But it happened that after a while Samson forgot his anger and began to miss his Philistine wife.

"I will go back to my wife's house," he said to himself, "and I will be her husband as I was before."

At the door of his wife's house, Samson met her father. The older man looked at the younger one in great surprise.

"What are you doing here, Samson?" he asked.

"I am not angry with your daughter any more," Samson answered, "and I have come to take her back as my wife."

The old man became so frightened, he could not say a word. But finally he spoke to Samson in a low voice. "I am sorry, but you cannot have your wife back."

"Why not?" shouted Samson.

"Because when you left, I thought you hated her. I was certain that you would never want to see

her again, so I let her marry another man."

Samson would not listen another minute. He could think of only one thing—*he could not have what he wanted*.

"I will punish the Philistines for this," he said. "And this time, I shall do them more harm than ever before!"

Then Samson ran out into the fields. He caught three hundred foxes and tied them together by their tails, two by two. And in the knot made by each pair of tails, he put a burning torch. Then he chased the foxes into the fields of the Philistines, where the grain was almost ready to be harvested. The torches set fire to the tall stalks of grain and burned them to the ground. From the grain fields the foxes ran among the olive trees, and the trees also burned to the ground.

14

"I Will Die With the Philistines"

With his great strength, Samson continued to do things to hurt the Philistines who ruled the land. He burned their fields, destroyed their trees, and killed their soldiers.

Once, after winning a battle against the Philistines, Samson decided to make his home in a town of the tribe of Judah. When the Philistines learned where Samson was, they sent soldiers to camp in the fields nearby.

The people of Judah were worried. "Why have you come as if to attack us?" they asked the Philistine soldiers.

The Philistines answered, "We have not come to attack you. We only want to capture Samson. If you give him to us, you will be safe."

So three thousand men of the tribe of Judah went to Samson and said, "Why did you bring these troubles upon us? Don't you know that the Philistines rule over us? Why do you fight against

them? Now the Philistines have ordered us to tie you with ropes and bring you to them, so that we may be safe from attack."

"Do as they have ordered," Samson said to the men of Judah. "Only make me one promise—that you will not try to harm me after I am tied up."

"We promise," said the men of Judah.

And they tied Samson's arms and hands with strong new ropes and brought him to the Philistines.

When the Philistines saw Samson standing before them, they gave a mighty cheer. But their joy did not last, for suddenly, with one quick movement, Samson broke the ropes that tied his arms and hands. And before the surprised Philistines knew what was happening, Samson had killed one thousand of them.

After this, Samson became a judge. He led the Israelites for twenty years, while the Philistines still ruled the land.

Then it happened that Samson fell in love again, this time with a woman named Delilah. When the leaders of the Philistines learned of this, they came to her and said, "If you can discover what makes Samson so strong and can tell us how to destroy his strength, we will give you money and make you very rich."

The next time Samson came to visit Delilah, she said to him, "If you love me, tell me your secret. What makes you so strong, and how can your strength be destroyed?"

"If someone were to tie me up with seven fresh bowstrings, I would lose my strength," Samson answered.

"I will try that," Delilah said, smiling.

Later, she got seven fresh bowstrings from the Philistine leaders.

After a few days, Delilah pretended that she was playing a game. "I have seven bowstrings," she told Samson in a teasing voice. And Samson let her tie him up with them. (He did not know that Philistine soldiers were hiding in the next room, waiting to capture him.)

When the strings were tight and all the knots were tied, Delilah called out, "The Philistines have come for you, Samson!"

Still thinking that this was a game, Samson stretched his powerful muscles. The bowstrings snapped and dropped to the ground.

Delilah tried again.

"Why did you hurt my feelings by telling me lies?" she asked Samson. "If you really love me, tell me the truth this time. *What makes you so strong, and how can your strength be destroyed?*"

And Samson said to Delilah, "The truth is that if someone were to tie me up with brand-new ropes, I would become as weak as any other man."

Again Samson let Delilah play her "game." This time she tied him up with brand-new ropes. And again, she called out with a laugh, "The Philistines have come for you, Samson!" And again Samson broke the ropes with which he was tied.

Delilah tried a third trick and once more Samson fooled her.

"How can I believe that you love me if you keep making fun of me?" Delilah scolded. "Three times you have lied to me!"

Day after day, Delilah kept asking Samson the very same questions. "What makes you so strong? How can your strength be destroyed?" Finally he could not stand her questions any more, and he told her the truth.

"My hair has never been cut off. That is the secret of my strength. If someone were to shave my head, I would become as weak as any other man."

This time Delilah knew that Samson was not teasing her. She sent a message to the Philistines, saying, "I have learned the secret that you want to know."

The Philistines came and brought the money they had promised Delilah.

Then, pretending that she loved Samson, Delilah sat down next to him and made him put his head in her lap. She spoke to him softly. Soon he fell fast asleep. When Delilah saw this, she signaled to a man who was hiding nearby. Without a sound, the man crept over to the sleeping Samson and cut off his hair.

"The Philistines have come for you, Samson!" Delilah called.

Sleepily, Samson opened his eyes. Philistine soldiers were standing all around him. Samson fought and fought, but without his hair, he had truly lost his strength! The Philistines captured Samson, put out his eyes, tied him with chains, and threw him into prison.

Now that they were free of Samson, the Philistines held a great celebration. Thousands came to the temple of the Philistine god, Dagon, to give thanks for the capture of Samson. They sang, danced, and shouted with joy. "Dagon has let us capture Samson! He has given us Samson, who was destroying our land and killing our people!"

And they sang, danced, and shouted some more. Then someone said, "Bring Samson from the prison. Let him stand before us so that we may laugh and make fun of this blind, weak fool!"

Samson was brought from his prison, and the crowd laughed and jeered and made fun of him.

Samson turned to the boy who had led him to the temple and spoke to him in a low voice. "You do not have to hold me by the hand any more. Just take me over to the pillars that are holding up the roof of this building, and I will lean on them."

The boy did as Samson asked. Then he walked away and left Samson alone between the pillars.

Standing before his enemies, Samson begged God for *one* favor. "O God," he prayed, "give me back my strength for just a short time, so that I may bring harm to the Philistines for blinding me!" Samson then put his hands on the two pillars that rose up on either side of him, and he pushed against them with all his might.

"I will die with the Philistines!" Samson cried. The roof of the temple came crashing to the ground, and all who had come to laugh at Samson were crushed under the falling building.

15

The Birth of Samuel

In the Bible, the Book of Samuel comes after the Book of Judges. Samuel was the last judge of Israel. Like Moses, Samuel was a very important *teacher* of the people. For many years, he traveled through the land reminding the Israelites to serve only the God of their Fathers and to follow His laws and commandments. He taught them what was right and wrong, and how God wanted them to act. The Jewish people have a special name for teachers like Moses and Samuel. They are called *prophets*.

In those days, the Israelites believed that God often spoke to the prophets and told them what to say to the people. They also believed that the prophets could sometimes tell what would happen in years to come, and that they knew secrets about the everyday world that ordinary people did not know—secrets such as where to find lost belongings. The people believed that all this knowledge came to the prophets from God.

Besides telling stories about the Prophet Samuel, the Book of Samuel also tells how the Israelite tribes finally defeated the enemies who had been attacking them for so long, and how at last they began to live in peace in Canaan, which was now the land of Israel.

Historians think that many parts of the Book of Samuel were written soon after the happenings they tell about, and that they describe these happenings correctly. They are "history." The Book of Samuel has more such history than the earlier books of the Bible.

But in Samuel, too, some parts of the stories about the important leaders of those days seem to be imaginary.

From the Book of Samuel

Elkanah, of the tribe of Levi, lived in the land of the tribe of Ephraim with his wife, Hannah. Elkanah loved his wife with all his heart, but Hannah was not happy. More than anything in the world, she wanted a child.

Once each year, Elkanah would go to the city of Shiloh to worship God and bring Him sacrifices.

There, in a beautiful, large tent called the Mishkan, Eli, the old priest, would take the sacrifices that the people brought, and burn them on the altar of God. (Only a priest was allowed to do this in the Mishkan.) In those days, the Israelites believed that God wanted such gifts.

Each year, Hannah went to Shiloh with her husband to pray that a child would soon be born to them, but her prayers were not answered.

Once, when Hannah felt that she could no longer bear her pain and sadness at not having a baby, she walked away from her husband and went to stand alone near the door of the Mishkan. Weeping bitterly, she made a promise to God. "If you give me a son, I will bring him here, so that he may live in the Mishkan all the days of his life and help the priest serve you."

As Hannah prayed, she did not notice that Eli, the priest, was watching her from his seat beside the door. Her lips moved and she wept, but she made no sound. Eli thought she was drunk.

"How long will you keep on drinking so much?" he asked her angrily.

"You are wrong," Hannah answered in a shaking voice. "I am not a drunken woman. I am only whispering to God of my sadness and begging Him to help me."

Then Eli spoke to her gently. "Go in peace," he said. "God will give you what you asked for."

Hannah's tears dried and she began to smile.

That year, a son was born to Hannah and Elkanah, and they called the baby Samuel.

When Samuel was about three years old, his mother and father brought him to the Mishkan in Shiloh. Hannah said to Eli, the priest, "I am the woman who once stood here begging God for a child. Here is the child I prayed for. I will give this child to God, as I promised. All his life, he will live at the Mishkan and help the priests."

Then Hannah hugged her little boy and put him into Eli's arms.

So it was that Samuel grew up in the Mishkan.

Once a year his parents visited him and brought him new clothes.

And Eli loved him and treated him like a son.

16

Samuel, the Last of the Judges

Eli had two sons who were also priests in the Mishkan, but they were not good men like their father. They stole meat from the animals that the Israelites brought as sacrifices to God. And when anyone said to them, "What you are doing is wrong," they answered, "If you do not give us what we want, we will take it by force."

When Eli heard how his sons were acting, he spoke to them. "This is not right, my sons," he said. "God will not forgive you."

But the young men paid no attention to their father's words, and he did nothing more to stop them.

One night, while the child Samuel was asleep in his room in the Mishkan, he heard a voice calling, "Samuel."

"Here I am," he said, sitting up in bed. He looked all around, but there was no one there. He ran to see what Eli wanted.

The old man looked at him in surprise. "I did not call you," he told the boy. "Go back and lie down."

So Samuel went back. And again the voice woke him, calling, "Samuel."

Again Samuel ran to Eli's room.

"Here I am, for you called me," he said to the priest.

"I did not call you, my son," Eli told him a second time. "Go, and try to sleep."

But the same voice called "Samuel" yet a third time, and once again Samuel ran to Eli.

Now Eli understood.

"Lie down in your bed," he said. "And if your name is called once more, you will know that it is the voice of God you hear. Then you are to say, 'Speak, O God, for I am listening.'"

So Samuel went to his room and waited. Again the call came: "Samuel, Samuel."

Trembling, Samuel whispered, "Speak, O God, for I am listening."

And God said to Samuel, "Because Eli did not stop his sons from doing wrong, I will bring great punishment upon him and upon them."

For the rest of that night, Samuel lay wide awake. He was too worried and frightened to sleep. The next morning he did not want to tell Eli what he had heard, but Eli would not let Samuel hide his secret. "You must tell me what God said to you," he demanded, so Samuel told him.

Eli's heart was sad. "God must do what He thinks is right," he said quietly.

Soon all of Israel knew that Samuel was a prophet of God.

When he became a young man, Samuel began to teach the people what was right and what was wrong. And he judged the Israelites for many years.

At this time, the Philistines ruled almost all of Canaan. They made life very hard for the Israelites, and the Israelites were worried. "We will be destroyed or driven from our lands," they said. Finally they turned to Samuel, their teacher, judge, and prophet.

"Help us," they cried.

"Do what I have taught you so many times," Samuel said, "and God will save you from the Philistines. Destroy the statues of gold, and silver, wood, and stone—the idols of Canaan that you worship as gods. Worship only the God of our Fathers, and walk in *His* ways."

The Israelites listened, and many changed their ways.

Samuel traveled back and forth throughout the lands of all the tribes, teaching the same lessons over and over again.

When Samuel grew older, he made his sons judges to help him in his work. But they were not wise and honest like their father. They loved money too much. They took bribes, and they often judged the people unfairly. The Israelites did not want them as leaders, and many worried about what would happen after Samuel died.

"Samuel will not be with us forever," they said. "Who will lead us and give us courage after he dies?"

Then the Israelites began to talk about a new idea. "If only we had a king to judge us, then we would be like all the other nations we know."

More and more Israelites began to think this was true. But where could they find such a king?

Samuel would know.

So the heads of the tribes of Israel came to Samuel and said, "Give us a king."

Samuel was not pleased. "God is the king of the Israelites. We need no other."

Then he said to the heads of the tribes, "This is what a king will do. He will take your sons to drive his chariots and ride his horses; to fight in his army and make weapons for his wars; and to plow his ground and reap his harvests. He will take your daughters to be cooks in his kitchens and bakers in his bakeries. He will take the animals from your flocks, the grain from your fields, the grapes from your vines, and the olives from your trees. You will all be his servants, and you will cry out for help because of the king you have chosen. But God will not listen to your cries."

Still the people would not change their minds.

"Give us a king," they said again, "so that we may be like all the other nations. Give us a king who will judge us, who will lead us in battle against our enemies!"

So God said to Samuel, "Give them a king."

17

A King is Chosen

In the tribe of Benjamin there lived a tall, handsome young farmer named Saul. One day some of his father's donkeys disappeared.

"Take one of our servant boys to help you, and go to look for the donkeys," Saul's father said to him.

And Saul did as his father asked.

He and the servant looked far and wide for several days, but they did not find the donkeys.

"Come," said Saul, "let us go back, for soon my father will stop worrying about the donkeys and start to worry about *us*."

"Wait," his servant answered. "I have heard that there is a famous seer in the city nearby—a man of God who knows secrets that ordinary people do not know. Let us go to him. Perhaps he can tell us where to find our donkeys." (At that time, a prophet was sometimes also called a seer.)

"A good idea," thought Saul. "But what gift can we bring to this seer?" he asked. "All our food is gone, and we have nothing else to give him."

"Look, I have a silver coin," said the servant, holding it up for Saul to see. "This will be our gift to the seer. Hurry now and let us look for him."

So they went to the city to find the seer. As they walked along, they saw a man coming toward them. They did not know that this was Samuel, the judge and prophet of Israel, the seer about whom Saul's servant had heard.

The day before, God had spoken to Samuel, saying, "Tomorrow I will send you a young man from the tribe of Benjamin. You will make him king over all the tribes of Israel. And he will save them from the Philistines."

And when Samuel saw Saul, God spoke again. "This is the man who will be king."

Saul walked up to the stranger. "Can you tell us where the house of the seer is?" he asked.

Samuel answered, "I am the seer you are looking for. Come and spend the night in my house. I have many things to tell you." Then he added, "And do not worry about your father's donkeys. They have been found."

So Saul and his servant spent the night in Samuel's house.

When the sun rose the next morning, Samuel woke Saul. "It is almost time for you to leave," he said to the young man.

Saul and Samuel walked, side by side, to the edge of the city. Saul's servant walked behind them.

Suddenly Samuel turned to Saul and said, "Tell your servant to walk ahead while we stay here. God has given me a message for you alone."

When the servant had left them, Samuel said to Saul, "This is what God has said: 'From this day on, Saul will be the king of all Israel.'

"And this is how you will know that what I have told you is true. Soon after you leave here, you will meet two men. They will say to you, 'The donkeys you are looking for have been found.' Then you will go farther, and you will meet three men: one carrying three baby goats, another carrying three loaves of bread, and a third carrying a bottle of wine. They will stop and offer you two loaves of bread. Take these from them.

"And when you go still farther—as far as the town where the Philistine soldiers are stationed —you will see a group of young men singing and playing musical instruments. They are prophets, teachers of the people. Through their songs, they remind the Israelites to stop worshiping the gods of Canaan, and to serve only the *one* God whose laws and commandments Moses taught our ancestors. Listen and you, too, will become a prophet and sing with these young men."

Samuel turned back to the city, and Saul went on his way. And everything happened just as Samuel had said.

Saul returned to his father's farm, but he told no one of Samuel's words.

Many days later, Samuel called the Israelites together and spoke to them. "Saul is the one whom God has chosen to be king."

And the people shouted, "Long live the king!"

A few scoffed and said, "How can this man save us?"

Saul heard their words but did not answer, and he showed no anger.

Samuel said to the Israelites, "Here is the king that you wanted. God has chosen him for you. If you and your king serve God and follow His laws, things will go well for you. But if you leave the ways of God and begin to worship the idols of Canaan again, both you and your king will be punished."

18

Living in Fear

One day some strangers came to the place where Saul lived. "We are from the tribe of Manasseh," they said, "from the city of Jabesh-Gilead, on the other side of the Jordan. Our neighbor, the king of Ammon, has made war on us. He has warned that he will destroy the whole city unless every man in Jabesh-Gilead lets his right eye be put out! We are not strong enough to save ourselves from Ammon. We need your help and the help of all the tribes of Israel."

When the people of Saul's city heard this news, they burst into tears. The air was filled with the sound of their weeping.

Just then Saul came back from the fields where he had been working.

"What has happened?" he asked, as he looked around at the sobbing men and women.

They told him about Jabesh-Gilead and the king of Ammon.

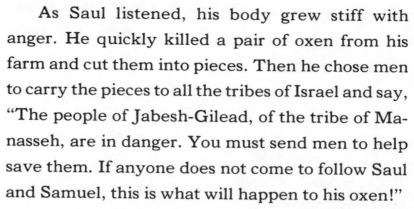

As Saul listened, his body grew stiff with anger. He quickly killed a pair of oxen from his farm and cut them into pieces. Then he chose men to carry the pieces to all the tribes of Israel and say, "The people of Jabesh-Gilead, of the tribe of Manasseh, are in danger. You must send men to help save them. If anyone does not come to follow Saul and Samuel, this is what will happen to his oxen!"

All through Canaan, the Israelites did what Saul, their king, asked. Men came from every tribe in the land, and Saul led them to the city that was under attack. They fought the soldiers of Ammon and chased them off, and the people of Jabesh-Gilead were saved.

In time, Saul, the farmer-king, gathered a small army around him—three thousand men who were always ready to protect the Israelites from those who might attack them. Jonathan, Saul's son, helped his father lead this army. The Israelite tribes were beginning to care for each other and to become one people again.

But one thing did not change, even after Saul became king. The Philistines still ruled over most of Canaan and made life as unhappy as ever for the Israelites.

One day Jonathan, the son of Saul, decided that the time had come to begin to free the Israelites from their Philistine rulers. He and a small group of Israelites attacked the Philistine soldiers who were stationed near their city. They defeated these soldiers, and chased them away.

When the battle was over, Saul sent men throughout the land to tell the Israelites about this first fight for their freedom. A new feeling of hope began to spread among the people, and men came from every tribe to help Saul try to push the Philistines out of the Israelite lands. Saul brought this army to Gilgal, a place in the land of the tribe of Benjamin. They waited there to see what the Philistines would do after their small defeat by Jonathan.

When the chiefs of the Philistines learned what Jonathan had done and what was happening at Gilgal, they decided to destroy those who were making trouble for them. So they sent chariots, and thousands of soldiers on foot to attack Saul and his men. The Philistines came into the land of the tribe of Benjamin and camped not far from the Israelites in Gilgal.

From their own camp the Israelites watched the Philistines gathering for the battle, and they lost their courage. How could they ever defeat this powerful army? Many who had come to fight ran away and hid in the caves and among the rocks of the nearby hills. Some even crossed the Jordan into the land of the tribe of Gad. "Perhaps the Philistines will not try to come this far," they thought.

But Saul stayed on in Gilgal. And some of the men stayed with him, though they, too, were afraid.

"We shall wait here for seven days," Saul said to his soldiers, "for Samuel promised to come on the seventh day to offer sacrifices to God and beg Him to help free us of the Philistines. Then we shall go into battle."

(In those times, people usually brought sacrifices to their gods before going to war. This was their way of asking the gods to help them. The Israelites also believed that this had to be done. They offered *their* sacrifices to the God of their Fathers.)

So the men waited, hoping each day that the Philistines would not decide to attack before Samuel arrived.

At last the seventh day came. But the hours moved on, and still Samuel had not come.

Now even the bravest of Saul's soldiers could no longer hide their fear. There was no more hope. The Philistines would surely destroy them. Some ran away to hide, as others had done before.

Saul waited and watched. Would he soon lose his whole army? Finally he could not wait any longer. The sacrifices had to be offered so that his men would stop being afraid.

"Bring me the animals to be sacrificed," he called out, and he offered them on the altar.

19

Jonathan and the Philistines

No sooner did Saul finish offering the sacrifices than Samuel appeared. Happy that the older man had come at last, Saul ran out to greet him.

But Samuel did not answer Saul's greeting. Instead he asked angrily, "Why did you do this?"

And Saul answered, "Because when you did not come, the people became very frightened. Some even ran away to hide. Fearing that the Philistines would soon attack us, I said to myself, 'We cannot go into battle without asking for God's help.' So I forced myself to offer the sacrifices."

Samuel listened silently. Then he looked into Saul's eyes and said, "You have done a foolish thing. I told you that I would come on this day to offer the sacrifices. You knew that this was what God wanted. But you, the king, were not patient! You did not wait! Because of this, you will not be king for long, and your son will not be king after you."

Samuel turned and walked away from Saul.

Saul went back to his camp and counted the men who were still there. Only about six hundred had stayed! Now Saul and Jonathan and this small, brave army waited for the attack they knew would soon come.

(The Israelite soldiers had few swords or spears, for, long before this, the Philistine rulers had said, "No Israelite may work with metal anywhere in Canaan—not even to sharpen tools such as plows and axes. For if we allow them to work with metal, they may secretly make swords or spears for their people to use against us." So the men in Saul's camp probably had bows and arrows, and slingshots with which to fight against the Philistines who came with their chariots and weapons of iron.)

Day after day Saul and his men watched and waited. When would the Philistines attack? Finally, Jonathan could wait no longer.

"Come," he whispered to the young man who helped him carry his weapons, "let us sneak over to the Philistine camp."

So the two of them slipped away and began to move across the valley to the mountain where the Philistines were camped. And nobody noticed that they were gone.

After climbing and creeping over the sharp and dangerous rocks, Jonathan suddenly stopped.

"Now let us go out into the open, where the Philistines will see us," he said to his helper. "If they call, 'Wait until we come over to you,' then we shall run away. But if they say, 'Come up to us,' that will be a sign that God will give them into our hands, and we shall go up to them."

So they stepped out into the open.

"Look," the Philistine soldiers said to each other, "the Israelites are beginning to creep out of their holes." And the Philistines shouted in teasing voices, "Come up to us, and we will show you something!"

"Did you hear their words?" Jonathan asked in great excitement. "Follow me." Then the two Israelites, like swift animals, fell upon a small group of laughing soldiers and killed twenty of them.

When the rest of the Philistines saw what had happened to their friends, they became so frightened that they could not even think clearly. Instead of trying to fight the two young Israelites, they ran away.

The Israelite watchmen, looking across from Saul's camp (as they did every minute of the day), suddenly saw a strange sight. Everywhere, Philistine soldiers were running! They ran this way and that, as if they did not know where to go or what to do.

Saul guessed what had happened.

"See who is gone from our camp," he said.

"Jonathan and his helper are missing," Saul was told.

"Let us go after them," he ordered.

When Saul and his small army came to the Philistine camp, they could hardly believe their eyes. Screaming Philistines were fighting each other wildly, like bitter enemies. Many were running away, leaving everything behind.

The Israelites who had been hiding in the nearby caves and rocks heard what was happening. They came out of their hiding places and joined Saul and his men to chase after the frightened Philistines.

In this way, the Israelites won their battle that day. But the Philistines remained strong, and they still ruled over most of the tribes of Israel.

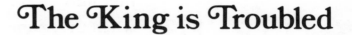

20

The King is Troubled

Saul, the farmer, had become Saul, the soldier-king. His life was filled with war and worry. He did not have a moment's peace.

Month after month, year after year, Saul fought to protect the Israelites from their enemies. Mostly he and his army fought against the Philistines. But other peoples also attacked from time to time, and they too had to be pushed back, too.

Israelites now came from every tribe in the land to join Saul's army. Slowly the separate tribes were becoming one people.

But Saul was growing tired. It seemed that the fighting would never end. This may have troubled him and made him sad, for he had been a man of peace—a farmer.

Another sadness lay hidden deep in his mind and heart. He had never spoken about it to anyone; yet he must have thought of it often. He knew that God was not pleased with him and would someday choose another king in his place. Samuel had told him this. Saul understood but still his heart ached, and sometimes anger burned within him like a fire. He could not stop these feelings when they came.

After a time, Saul's family and friends began to notice that he was acting strangely. Every once in a while he looked around him like a trapped animal. His body trembled, and his face turned dark with fear. At such moments he often screamed with anger. But soon the fear and anger passed, and Saul again became the man they knew and loved.

"Let us find a musician who knows how to play beautiful music on the strings of the harp," Saul's friends suggested. "And whenever terrible feelings come upon you, he will play for you, and his music will bring you peace."

"Find me such a man," Saul agreed.

One of the young men spoke. "In the city of Bethlehem there is a shepherd named David, son of Jesse, who plays the harp. Perhaps he can help the king."

So Saul sent messengers to Jesse saying, "Send me your son, David."

And David came to Saul, and Saul loved him very much.

Whenever the fear and anger came upon Saul, David played beautiful music on his harp, and the king soon felt well again.

Although David was now Saul's musician, he still had to help care for his father's sheep from time to time. So he went back and forth, staying sometimes with his own family and sometimes in Saul's household.

21

David and Goliath

Soon there was war again with the Philistines.

Both the Israelites and the Philistines were getting ready for a great battle. The Philistines were camped on one mountain; and across from them, on another mountain, was the Israelite camp. Between them lay a deep valley.

Among the Philistines there was a powerful warrior, a giant named Goliath. His head was covered with a helmet of metal, his body with a suit of metal armor, and in his hand he carried a spear with a metal tip.

One morning Goliath walked to the edge of the Philistine camp and stood where the Israelites could see him.

"Why should all our soldiers fight each other?" he shouted across the valley. "Is it not better that only one Philistine and one Israelite fight? I will fight for the Philistines, and you choose a man who will fight for the Israelites. If the Israelite kills me, the Philistines shall be your servants. But if I kill him, you Israelites will be our servants, and we will rule over you."

Then Goliath laughed a long, loud laugh, for he was sure that no Israelite soldier would have the courage to fight him.

And he was right. When the Israelites heard what the giant wanted, they were filled with fear. Nobody dared step forward.

Every morning and every evening, for many days, Goliath shouted the same challenge across the valley that separated the two armies. And each time, he laughed longer and louder at the frightened Israelites.

It happened that three of David's brothers were in Saul's army at this time. And one day Jesse, their father, became worried about them.

"Go to the Israelite camp and find your brothers," he said to David, who was at home caring for the sheep. "Ask if they are well, and give them these gifts of food."

And Jesse gave David roasted grain and bread to take to his brothers.

Early the next morning, David started out for the mountain where Saul and his men were camped. It was almost evening when he arrived, and he immediately began to look for his brothers. After a while he found them and said, "Our father wants to know how you are, and he sends these gifts of food for you."

As he stood and talked with his brothers, David suddenly heard a rumbling laugh. Then a voice boomed across the valley: "What are you waiting for? Why do you not choose an Israelite to come out and fight against me? Is it because you are all afraid?"

David's face became hot with anger. "Who is that one, who laughs and makes fun of us?" he asked.

"That is Goliath, the Philistine giant," answered some men, with fear in their voices.

David grew even more angry. "We cannot let him laugh at us and put us to shame. Someone must stop him!" he cried.

Before long, a messenger from Saul approached.

"The king has been told what you said about Goliath," he told David. "The king would like to speak with you."

David followed the messenger to Saul's tent, the sound of Goliath's laughter still ringing in his ears.

"We must show this Philistine that we are not afraid of him. *I* will go out and fight against him!" David said to the king.

Saul stared at David. "You cannot go," he protested. "Goliath is a much better warrior than you. He has been fighting almost all his life. He will surely kill you."

But David would not be stopped. "Sometimes," he replied, "when I am out in the pasture with my father's sheep, a lion or bear takes one of the lambs and runs away. Whenever this happens, I chase after the lion or bear and kill him and save my father's lamb. Today I will do the same with Goliath. God will protect me from him, as He has protected me from the wild animals."

Saul listened quietly until David had finished speaking. "Go, and may God help you," he said.

Then, Saul dressed David in his own armor—a suit of metal to cover his body, and a helmet of metal to cover his head. And in David's hand, Saul placed his sword.

"I cannot wear the armor and helmet, for I am not used to them," David said.

David took off the heavy metal suit and helmet, laid aside the king's sword, and slipped back into his own shepherd's clothing.

Then he left the tent, went to a stream that flowed beside the Israelite camp and carefully picked out five smooth stones. He dropped these into the shepherd's sack that hung from his waist. In his hand he carried a slingshot.

And David walked out to meet the Philistine giant. Goliath also began to walk. The two came closer and closer together. Finally they could see one another clearly across the valley that separated their camps.

Goliath looked, rubbed his eyes, and looked again. Then he almost exploded with anger.

"Are *you* the one the Israelites sent?" he roared. "Where are your weapons? Do you plan to hit me with sticks as if I were a dog?"

After a moment, his voice changed. "Come —come toward me," he teased, "and I will kill you."

David stood perfectly still. "I am not afraid of you or your dangerous weapons," he answered, "for I know that God will save us from you."

Goliath said no more. The two men again began to move toward each other. David put his hand into his shepherd's bag, took out a stone, and placed it in his slingshot. Taking careful aim, he let the stone go. It flew through the air and struck Goliath in the forehead.

The Philistine giant fell to the ground, dead.

The battle was over. Now it was the Philistines who feared the Israelites. Too frightened to fight, they ran from their camp, leaving behind their tents, their weapons, and everything they had brought with them.

The news was carried to every tribe in the land. "Goliath is dead! A young shepherd named David killed him with a stone from his slingshot!"

And wherever Saul and David passed, as they made their way back to the home of the king, women came out to sing and dance and play music in their honor.

"Saul is great. But David is even greater," they sang.

Saul listened and said nothing, but his heart pounded in his chest, and his hands tightened into hard fists. "Soon they will want to make David king in my place," he said to himself. From then on, Saul did not trust David.

22

"David Must Die"

Saul grew more and more unhappy. Whenever he thought of how much the people loved David, he became wild with jealousy. After a while, everyone close to the king could see that his old sickness had returned. But now David's music did not make Saul well, for Saul's love for the young man had turned to hate. Sometimes he could hardly bear to look at David.

Once, when David was playing his harp for Saul, the troubled king suddenly threw a spear at him. But David jumped aside and was not hurt.

Another time, Saul had a new idea for getting rid of David.

"You have seen my daughter Merav," he said. "I will give her to you as your wife. But first you must go out with my army and fight against the Philistines. Then I will know that you are brave enough to be the king's son-in-law."

And Saul thought to himself, "If I send David into battle, I will not have to harm him with my own hands. He will be killed by the Philistines instead."

But to Saul's great surprise, David answered, "I cannot marry your daughter. I am just an ordinary man. I am not important enough to be the son-in-law of the king."

So Merav married another man.

Saul had a second daughter, named Michal, who happened to love David very much.

And Saul said to himself, "Perhaps my plan will still work. Maybe David will agree to fight against the Philistines if I promise him my daughter Michal as a bride."

So Saul called some of his servants and commanded: "Speak with David secretly. Tell him that you have heard how much I want him to be my son-in-law. Tell him also that he is loved by all who work for the king. Tell him that everyone in the king's household hopes he will marry Michal, the king's daughter."

Saul's servants spoke to David as the king had ordered, but David was still not ready to change his mind.

"I am a poor man," he said. "I cannot give Saul

the money and the gifts that a bridegroom must pay when he marries the daughter of the king."

(In those days, every bridegroom had to give money or gifts to the father of his bride.)

When Saul's servants brought him David's answer, he was happy. At last he knew the real reason David would not marry either of his daughters.

"Go back to David," Saul said to his servants, "and say to him: 'The king does not want money or gifts from you. He asks only that you attack one of the places where Philistine soldiers are stationed on Israelite land. If you win that battle and free the place of Philistine soldiers, the king will be pleased to have you as his son-in-law.'"

"This time," thought Saul, "David will do as I ask. But he will not be able to defeat the Philistines. They are too strong for him. He will never come back."

But things did not go as Saul planned. David *did* defeat the Philistine soldiers. He came home safely, and Saul had to let him marry his daughter Michal, as he had promised.

Saul's mind grew more and more troubled. "David must die!" he mumbled over and over to himself.

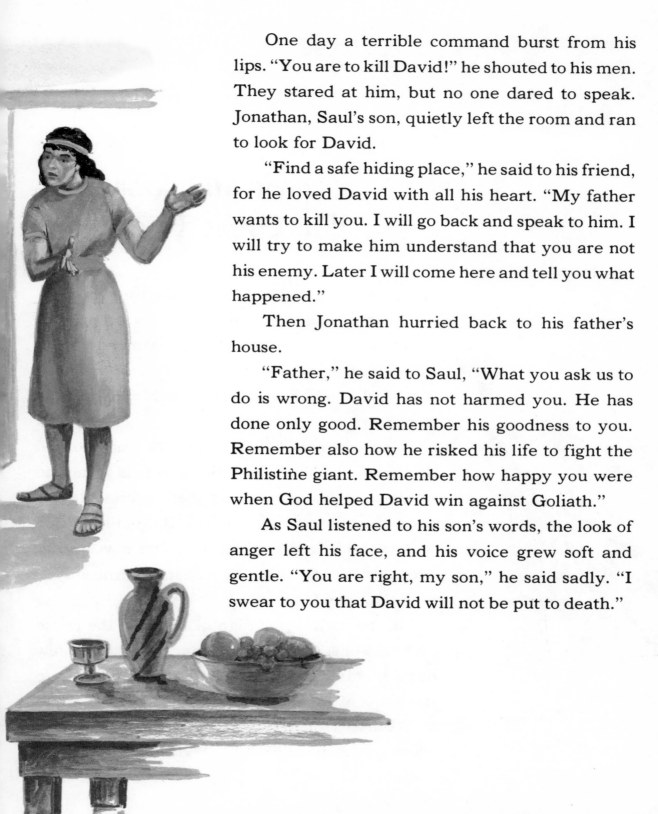

One day a terrible command burst from his lips. "You are to kill David!" he shouted to his men. They stared at him, but no one dared to speak. Jonathan, Saul's son, quietly left the room and ran to look for David.

"Find a safe hiding place," he said to his friend, for he loved David with all his heart. "My father wants to kill you. I will go back and speak to him. I will try to make him understand that you are not his enemy. Later I will come here and tell you what happened."

Then Jonathan hurried back to his father's house.

"Father," he said to Saul, "What you ask us to do is wrong. David has not harmed you. He has done only good. Remember his goodness to you. Remember also how he risked his life to fight the Philistine giant. Remember how happy you were when God helped David win against Goliath."

As Saul listened to his son's words, the look of anger left his face, and his voice grew soft and gentle. "You are right, my son," he said sadly. "I swear to you that David will not be put to death."

23

David and Jonathan: The Great Friendship

But Saul could find no peace. Each time the sickness came upon him, he forgot his promise to Jonathan, and the old thought started racing through his mind: "David must die! David must die!" It drove him wild and made him do terrible things.

One afternoon, Saul again did what he had done many weeks before. He raised his spear and threw it at David, who sat before him playing restful music to make him well. Again, David jumped aside and was not hurt, but now he was sure that his life would be in danger if he stayed with Saul any longer.

In the darkness of night, David left the house and made his way to a different city. After a few days, he came out of his hiding place and went to the home of Jonathan, his dearest friend.

"What wrong have I done, that your father should want to kill me?" David asked. He told

Jonathan what Saul had tried to do. Jonathan could not believe what he heard.

"It cannot be true that my father wants to kill you," he said. "He never does anything, large or small, without telling me first. If he meant to do this dreadful thing, why would he not have spoken to me about it?"

David felt sorry for his friend. "Your father knows how much you like me. He did not want to upset you and make you sad. Perhaps that is why he did not tell you."

Tears filled Jonathan's eyes. "Tell me what to do, and I will do it for you," he said to David.

David thought for a moment and then said to his friend, "Tomorrow is the Festival of the New Moon, and the king will have a feast at his house as he does every month. He expects me to be at this feast. But I will not come. Instead, I will hide in that field until the night after tomorrow." And David pointed to the field where he planned to hide.

"You, of course, will go to the feast. And if your father asks why I am not at the table, say to him, 'David begged my permission to visit his family for a few days, so I let him go.' Then watch the king carefully and listen to his words. If he says, 'You did well,' we will know that he means me no harm. But if Saul grows angry, that will be our sign that he wants to destroy me."

Suddenly David's voice changed. "Perhaps you, too, believe that I have done something wrong and deserve to die," he said to Jonathan. "If you do, then kill me yourself, I beg you."

Jonathan shuddered and covered his face with his hands. He stood that way for a long time. Then he raised his head and looked long and hard at the friend whom he loved like a brother. At last the words came.

"I promise that I will tell you the truth about what happens at the feast," he said.

For a while the two men were very quiet. Each was thinking his own thoughts. Jonathan broke the stillness.

"Now I must ask you to make *me* a promise," he said to David. "Someday you will become king in my father's place. When that happens, please show kindness to me and my family."

And David promised.

Then Jonathan spoke and said, "In three days, I will take my bow and arrows and come out to the field that you have shown me. I will bring a young boy with me to help carry the arrows. In the field, I will pretend to aim at something I see. I will shoot three arrows into the air. Then I will ask the boy to look for them and bring them back to me. When he

begins to run, you must listen carefully to the words I say. If I call after the boy, 'You have gone too far. The arrows fell somewhere behind you,' that will mean that you are safe. But if I shout, 'Go further. You have not yet reached the arrows,' you will know that your life is in danger."

The next night, the king came to the festival table. From his seat by the wall, he looked around the room. Everyone was there but David, whose place was empty. Saul said nothing.

"Maybe David was unable to come today," he thought to himself. "I will see what happens tomorrow, when we have another feast."

The second night, David's place was still empty. This time, Saul decided to speak.

"Why did David not come today? And where was he yesterday?" he asked his son.

And Jonathan answered, "David begged my permission to visit his family for a few days, so I let him go. That is why he is not here."

Saul's face turned red as fire.

"You, too, are against me," he roared. "You know well that if David lives, *he* will become king instead of you. Yet you choose to be his friend. I command you to bring him to me, for he deserves to die!"

Jonathan spoke softly. "Why should David be put to death? What has he done?" he asked.

At this, Saul lifted his spear as if to throw it at his own son.

Now Jonathan knew the truth. Furious, he jumped up from the table and ran out of the room.

The next morning Jonathan went to the field where David was hiding. Beside him walked a small boy—the one who would hunt for his arrows.

Jonathan said to the boy, "Run, and find the arrows that I shoot." As the boy ran, Jonathan shot some arrows far over his head.

When the boy came near the place where the arrows had landed, Jonathan called out, "Go further. You have not yet reached the arrows."

The boy went further, found the arrows, and brought them back to Jonathan. Then Jonathan handed him his bow and all his arrows and said, "Take these to the city for me. I will come in a while."

As soon as the boy had gone, David stepped out of his hiding place and bowed low before his friend. The two men threw their arms around each other and began to cry.

"Go," Jonathan whispered to David, "and let there be peace between your family and mine."

24

The Outcast

Where could David go? Where would he be safe from the soldiers that Saul might send to hunt for him? Surely not among the Israelite tribes. Among the Philistines? It was dangerous, but he would try. David made his way to the Philistine city of Gath. But as soon as he entered the city he was taken before the king.

"Is this not David, the hero of the Israelites?" the Philistines said to the king of Gath.

David was frightened. Had he escaped from Saul only to be killed by the Philistines?

Then he had an idea. He would pretend to be crazy. Maybe that would fool the Philistines, and they would think they had made a mistake. Looking like a wild man, David began to run back and forth—his hair flying in the wind, his tongue hanging out of his mouth, and saliva dripping down his beard.

"Why do you bring me this crazy man?" the king of Gath scolded. "Have I not enough madmen of my own here?"

And the Philistines chased David out of Gath.

From then on, David lived like a hunted animal—in caves, among rocks, in forests, anywhere he could feel safe. After a time, other men who needed to hide gathered around him—about six hundred of them in all—and he became their leader.

To keep alive, David and his men often did cruel things. They stole food from the fields of peaceful farmers, and animals from the flocks of peaceful shepherds. Without stealing, they might have starved to death.

But they did not always steal. Sometimes they went to the homes of the rich and *asked* for supplies.

One such man was Nabal, the husband of Abigail.

Nabal was very rich. He had three thousand sheep and a thousand goats. For many weeks, his shepherds pastured the animals in the wilderness where David and his men happened to be living. When it was time to shear the wool from the sheep so that it could be made into cloth, Nabal's

shepherds led their flocks back to their master's town.

David picked ten young men from among those who were with him and said, "Go to the home of Nabal and say to him, 'Peace to you. We bring this message from our leader, David: 'Nabal, for a long time your shepherds pastured your flocks near the place where my men and I made our home. We could have hurt your shepherds, but we did not. We could have stolen your animals, but we did not. Ask your young men, and they will tell you that what we are saying is true. And so, because we did not harm you, we ask you now to be good to us. Please give us whatever gifts you can.'"

When Nabal heard this message, he answered angrily, "Why does this David of yours think that he and his men are so important? Why should I send him gifts of bread and water and meat?"

And he would not give a thing to David's men.

When David heard what Nabal had said, he became furious.

"Four hundred of you are to come with me to Nabal's house," he said, "while the rest stay here to guard the supplies we have."

So four hundred of David's men set out with their leader.

Meanwhile, at Nabal's house, one of the young shepherds was speaking to Abigail, Nabal's wife.

"A short while ago, David sent messengers to ask our master for gifts, but Nabal spoke to them in a very angry way and sent them away with nothing.

"Abigail, it is important for you to understand that David and his men were very good to us in the wilderness. Not only did they not hurt us or steal from us, but they protected us from others who would have attacked our flocks.

"Now you must act quickly. Otherwise, David and his men will surely come here and do harm to all of us, because of the ugly way our master treated them."

As soon as the shepherd had finished speaking, Abigail began to give orders to the other shepherds around her. In a short while, they had gathered two hundred loaves of bread, two large containers of wine, the meat of five sheep, much grain, and many raisins and figs. They loaded all this onto the backs of donkeys.

Then Abigail said to some of the shepherds, "Let us go." She climbed on her donkey and set out to meet David. She did not tell her husband, Nabal, what she was doing.

On a twisting mountain road, Abigail saw David and his men coming toward her. She quickly slipped from her donkey and ran to meet them. Bowing before David, she said, "Listen to my words, I beg you. Pay no attention to my husband, Nabal. He is not a good person. If *I* had seen your messengers when they came, I would have sent you the gifts that you deserve. And now, let these presents that I have brought be given to the men who follow you."

And David said to Abigail, "I thank God who sent you to me this day. You stopped me from spilling the blood of innocent people. For if you had not come, I, in my anger, would have killed every man in Nabal's household."

Then David took the gifts that Abigail had brought, and she went back to her husband's house.

The next morning, Abigail told Nabal all that had happened. He was so upset that he became very sick. Shortly after that he died.

When David heard that Nabal was dead, he sent messengers to Abigail to ask her to be his wife. (In those days, a man was allowed to have many wives.) Abigail followed the messengers into the wilderness and married David.

25

The King is Spared

Once, when David was making his home in the wilderness of Ein-Gedi, somebody saw him and said to Saul, "David is in Ein-Gedi."

When Saul heard this, he could not rest. Taking three thousand of his best soldiers, he led them into the wilderness to search for David. As the day wore on, Saul became tired and stopped in a cave to rest. He lay on the floor of the cave and fell fast asleep. He did not know that many eyes were watching him. Deep within that cave were David and his followers. From their dark hiding place, they could see the sleeping king.

"Now you can kill Saul," David's men said to him, "as he would kill you."

David did not answer. Instead he took his knife and crept toward the sleeping Saul. With one fast stroke, he cut a piece of cloth from the bottom of Saul's robe and quickly moved away.

David would not hurt Saul.

When Saul awoke and left the cave, David followed.

"My king!" David called.

Saul turned his head.

There, not far away was David, bowing to the ground before him!

And David said to Saul, "Why do you believe that I want to hurt you? Why do you not understand that I am your friend?"

Then David held up the piece of cloth he had cut from Saul's robe. "Look at this, my king. Look, and you will know that I was right beside you in the cave. I could have killed you. But there is no hate in my heart for you, and I shall never harm you —as I did not harm you today!"

When David finished speaking, Saul burst into tears. "My son," he cried, "you are a far better person than I. May God be good to you because of your goodness to me. And now, I must ask one more kindness of you. I know that one day soon you will be king in my place. Please promise that when that time comes, you will not hurt my family."

David promised and Saul left.

But David knew that he was still not safe. He knew that the sickness would come upon Saul again, as it had so many times before. When it did, the king would try again to kill him. So David and his followers stayed in the wilderness.

Saul's fear and anger did come back, and once more the old thought filled Saul's mind day and night: "David must die!" And for the second time Saul went to the wilderness to hunt for the young man he had once loved as a son.

When David learned that Saul had come, he sent spies to see where the king and his men were camped. The spies found the place and told David exactly where it was.

Late that night, David decided to see the camp for himself. With a few of his closest friends, he set out in the darkness. Before long, they came to the top of a hill near Saul's camp. Looking down, they saw that everyone in the camp was asleep. The men lay on the ground in one large circle. In the center slept Saul, his spear stuck in the ground near his head. Next to him was Abner, the general of the army. All around them were the soldiers. No guards watched over the camp, and no sleeping man stirred.

"Who will go down to the camp with me?" David whispered.

"I will," said Abishai, one of his friends.

Quiet as shadows, they went down the hillside and slipped into Saul's camp. No one woke up. No one tried to stop them. They passed through the sleeping circle and stood beside the king.

"God has given Saul into your hands," Abishai said with joy. "Let me kill him with his own spear."

But David would not let Abishai touch the king. "No," he said, "God will take Saul's life in His own way. *We* shall take only his spear and his jug of water and leave in peace."

And that is what they did.

Then, David climbed to a spot high above Saul's camp. His voice rang out through the night. "Awaken, men of Saul!" And he called to Saul's general, "Abner, Abner, answer me!"

Abner stirred. "What is it?" he asked. "Who disturbs the king?"

David laughed loudly. "You are called a brave soldier in Israel; you are called a great man. Why did you not protect your king tonight? Why did you not see us when we came into your camp to kill him?

"Look around. Where is Saul's spear? Where is the jug of water that stood near his head?"

Awakened by the noise, Saul recognized David's voice.

"Is it you I hear, David, my son?"

"It is I, my king," David answered. Then he said to Saul, "What wrong have I done that you chase after me again and again? Why must I hide among strangers? Why may I not serve God among my own people?"

Saul cried out, as he had done before, "I have sinned!"

His voice grew softer. "Come back, David, my son. As you did not harm me this night, so will I not harm you. I know now how foolish I have been to think you were my enemy."

But David was more certain than ever that he could not go home as long as Saul was alive. So he said, "Here is the king's spear. Let someone come and get it."

Then he turned and went his own way.

26

Saul's Last Battle

Throughout the years that he was king, Saul fought many battles against the Philistines, and he forced them out of many of the Israelite lands over which they ruled. But the Philistine leaders would not give up. Again and again they sent armies to attack the cities and towns of Israel.

All the while, Saul's sickness grew worse. His mind and heart were seldom at peace. At last his strength left him, and he felt that he could no longer hope to rid his people of this powerful enemy. But still he went on fighting the Philistine armies.

Then came the battle Saul feared. Thousands of Philistine soldiers poured into the land of the Israelites to attack Saul's army. When the Israelite soldiers saw how strong the Philistines were, they were afraid and ran away. Saul and his sons ran too, but they could not escape. The Philistines caught Saul's sons and killed them, and Saul, the first king of Israel, died on that day also.

Once more, the Philistines ruled over most of the Israelite lands.

When David, in his place of hiding, heard the news of the battle, he wept bitterly for Saul whom he pitied, and for Jonathan whom he loved. And he sang a song of tears:

Your great men have fallen, O Israel.
Saul and Jonathan—
Lovely and pleasant in their lives—
And in their death, they were not separated.
They were faster than eagles.
They were stronger than lions.
Your great men have fallen!

David's life was no longer in danger, so he left his hiding place and went to live in Hebron, a city of the tribe of Judah. The people of Judah made David their king, and he ruled in Hebron for seven years.

Then people from the rest of the tribes of Israel came to David and said, "Be our king also." So David became king over all the tribes of Israel, as Saul had been before him.

Like Saul, David did not worship the gods of Canaan. And, like Saul, David fought against the enemies of Israel. But David succeeded where Saul had failed. He drove the Philistines back to their cities along the coast, and he fought against other kings who sometimes made war on the tribes of Israel.

And David captured the city of Jerusalem and made it his home. From that time onward, Jerusalem was called "the City of David."

At long last, the tribes of Israel had become one people, ruled by one king, living in peace in its own land.

27

David and Bathsheba

Late one afternoon, David went up on the roof of his house to enjoy the cool mountain air of Jerusalem. Looking down, he could see the whole city, for the king's house stood on the highest spot in Jerusalem.

As David walked slowly and lazily around the roof, his eyes wandered over homes and court-yards. He loved to look at the city.

Suddenly David stopped. On the roof of a nearby house he saw a woman. She was very beautiful, and he stood watching her for a long time.

Later, David asked some of his servants if they knew who this woman was.

"That is Bathsheba, whose husband, Uriah, is away fighting in the king's army," one of the servants answered.

"The wife of Uriah," David said slowly, as if talking to himself.

Now he knew that Bathsheba was a married woman. And one of the Ten Commandments teaches that it is wrong to take away another person's husband or wife. But at that moment, these things did not seem to matter to David. He could think only one thought: "I must have that beautiful woman as my wife!"

David sent a letter to Joab, the general of his army, saying:

In the next battle, put Uriah in a very dangerous spot—in front of the best soldiers of the enemy. Then have all the Israelite soldiers move back. Let him stand alone, so that he will be killed.

When Joab read this letter, he was not troubled by the king's order. If that was what David wanted, then that was what his general must do. Joab placed Uriah in the most dangerous spot he could find, and Uriah fell in the battle.

Then Joab sent a messenger to tell David about the fighting and to say, "Uriah is dead."

A few weeks later, David sent for Bathsheba and she became one of his many wives. Before long, a son was born to David and Bathsheba. *But what David had done made God very angry. It was wrong. It was not how God wanted the Israelites to act.*

God sent Nathan, the prophet, to David. And Nathan said to the king, "I must tell you a story about something that happened:

Two men lived in the same city. One was rich and the other poor. The rich man owned many sheep, goats, cows, and oxen. But the poor man owned only one little lamb. He had bought it when it was very young, and it grew up with his family. It ate from the man's dish and drank from his cup. The lamb was his pet. Sometimes he held it lovingly in his arms. It was as dear to him as his own children.

One day a traveler stopped at the house of the rich man, and the rich man said to himself, 'I must prepare meat for my guest. But I hate to use an animal from my own flock.' So he stole the poor man's lamb, killed it, and cooked its meat for his guest.

David listened carefully to every word that Nathan spoke, and when he heard the end of the story, he became very angry.

"That rich man deserves to die for what he did!" cried David.

Nathan waited until David's anger had passed. Then, pointing his finger at the king, he said, "You are the man! God gave you so much. He saved you from Saul. He made you king. You have wives, children, a beautiful house, and all sorts of riches. Why, then, did you do something hateful to God? Why did you have Uriah killed and take his wife for yourself? Because you acted this way, God will punish you in many ways for as long as you live."

A shiver shook David's body and he closed his eyes tightly as if he were in pain. In a hoarse voice he whispered, "What I did was wrong. I have sinned against God."

Nathan spoke again. "You, David, will live, but the baby that was born to you and Bathsheba will die." Nathan turned away and left the king. Nathan's words came true, and the baby died.

28

A House to Honor God

When the king of the neighboring city of Tyre heard that David had become king of all the Israelites, he asked his woodsmen to cut down many cedar trees in his forests. He sent these as a gift to David. (Cedar wood is especially strong and beautiful.) Along with the trees, the king of Tyre also sent carpenters who knew how to make lovely things out of wood, and masons who knew how to make beautiful things out of stone. They built a house for David—a palace for the new king.

David thanked his friend, the king of Tyre, for this wonderful present. But most of all, he thanked God for helping him become king of Israel.

"Only one thing is missing now," David thought to himself. "The Ark that holds the Ten Commandments is standing in a far-away city. We must bring it here, to Jerusalem."

So David called together thirty thousand people—all the leaders of Israel—and went with them to bring the Ark to Jerusalem. When they came to the Ark, men of the tribe of Levi lifted it carefully and carried it on their shoulders.

In their happiness, the people who had come with David danced and sang and played musical instruments all the way back to Jerusalem. David, too, danced and shouted with joy before the Ark.

At last, the Ark reached Jerusalem. It was placed in a large tent that David had set up for it.

But David felt troubled.

"Look at my palace," he said to Nathan, the prophet and teacher in Israel. "It is much more beautiful than the tent where the Ark of God stands."

"Do as your heart tells you," Nathan said to David. For he saw how much David wanted to build a lovely house for the Ark.

The next morning, however, Nathan rushed back to the palace. He said to David, "I heard the voice of God last night, saying, 'Go and tell this to David: *You* are not to build a house for the Ark. Your son, who will be king after you will build this house.'"

Many years later, when David knew that he would not live much longer, he called his son Solomon and explained to him God's reason for this.

"With all my heart, I wanted to build a beautiful house for the Ark, but God would not let me do this because I was not a man of peace. God said to me, 'You have fought many battles and have spilled much blood. That is why I do not want you to build a house for the Ark. However, after you are gone, there will be peace and quiet in the land of Israel. Your son, who will rule after you, will not have to go to war. He will spill no blood. *He* will build a house in My honor.'"